Robert W Moffatt

The Apprentices' Guide

Or, every lady her own pastry cook and confectioner

Robert W Moffatt

The Apprentices' Guide
Or, every lady her own pastry cook and confectioner

ISBN/EAN: 9783744793148

Printed in Europe, USA, Canada, Australia, Japan

Cover: Foto ©Lupo / pixelio.de

More available books at **www.hansebooks.com**

THE

Apprentices' Guide

OR,

Every Lady Her Own Pastry Cook

AND

CONFECTIONER.

BY

ROBERT W. MOFFATT,

Practical Cake Baker and Confectioner.

WEST CHESTER:
HICKMAN & HAMMOND, PUBLISHERS.
1869.

PREFACE.

The Author, when an apprentice, needing greatly information regarding his business, that information which could be relied upon, and such that the inexperienced might follow with confidence and success, resolved at that time, if he should ever acquire at any future time the knowledge requisite, he would publish a Receipt Book containing reliable information, and now after twenty years of practical experience he presents the receipts herein contained as the best he has ever used and the only ones used by him at the present time.

R. W. M.

PASTRY.

To make fine Puff Pastry, take equal parts of Butter and Flour: Take 1 pound of Flour, put half in your pan and the other half on the table; then take 1 pound of Butter, wash it well in ice water until you have all the salt washed out; then spread it about 1 inch thick on a pan, and put it on the ice to harden; when hard, cut it into four parts; put one-fourth into your pan with the flour, cut it in very small pieces with a knife, mix it with cold water to the consistency of bread dough, being careful not to stir it too much. After having mixed it, roll it out very thin with your rolling pin, take another portion of your butter, divide it in small pieces all over the surface of your pastry. Sprinkle it with flour; then double it four times, roll it again and take another portion of your butter, and do with it as before; so continue until you have used it all, being careful to save enough flour to roll it out with. When you are ready to bake, after having all the butter in, cut it into four parts; having done so, roll each part up very tight, lay them on a pan and put in a cool place; when it becomes cold, cut off as much as you think proper to cover your plate, roll it very thin, sprinkle some flour over it, double it four times, roll it out about one-eighth of an inch thick, cover your plate, trim off the edge with a sharp knife, and bake in a brisk oven.

ANOTHER.—Take 1 pound of butter, wash it well, spread it on a pan, place it on the ice to harden; when hard, have ready 1 pound of flour, cut your butter up very fine in it, mix with cold water the same as before, put it on your table, dust it with flour, give it one roll with your rolling pin ; then double it four times, put it away to get cold; when you are to use it roll the same as in first receipt. This is best to work on board of Steamboats.

Common Pastry.

1 pound of flour, ¾ pound of lard, ¼ ounce of salt, ½ pint of cold water.

Rub your lard and salt in your flour with your hands, when well mixed put in your water and stir it with a knife to make dough.   This is ready for immediate use.

Lemon Pudding.

1¼ pounds of butter, 1¼ pounds of sugar—pulverized, 1 pint of egg yellows, 3 lemons—the grated rind and juice, 1 wine glass of brandy.

Beat the butter and sugar very light, whisk the yellows up very light, mix the eggs into the butter and sugar at four times ; when all your eggs are in add the lemon rind and juice, and last the brandy.

Cocoanut Pudding.

½ pound of butter, ¾ pound of sugar—pulverized, ½ pint of egg whites, ¾ pound of grated cocoanut.

Beat the butter and sugar very light, then mix in the egg whites, half at a time; when the eggs are all in stir in lightly the cocoanut.

Pumpkin Pudding.

1 pound of butter, 1½ pounds of sugar—crushed or B, 1½ pounds of pumpkin, 12 whole eggs, 1 wine glass of brandy, nutmeg and cinnamon to taste.

Have the pumpkin ready boiled and passed through a cullender, then beat the butter and sugar light, add the eggs three at a time ; when the eggs are all in put in the brandy and last your pumpkin with the spice.

Apple Pudding.

¾ pound of apples, ¾ pound of butter, 1 pound of sugar—

crushed or B, 10 whole eggs, nutmeg or lemon rind flavor.

Pare and grate the apples, beat the butter and sugar light, then add the eggs 5 at a time ; when the eggs are all in stir in the apples and flavor.

Dried Apple Flourendines

Are made in the same way, but the apples must be boiled and passed through a cullender, using 8 eggs and brown sugar with a wine glass of brandy.

Sweet Potato Pudding.

$1\frac{1}{2}$ pounds of sweet potato, $\frac{3}{4}$ pound of butter, $\frac{3}{4}$ pound of B sugar, 12 whole eggs, 1 wine glass of brandy, cinnamon or nutmeg flavor.

Pare, boil and pass the potatoes through a cullender, beat the buter and sugar light, then add the eggs, 4 at a time ; when the eggs are all in stir in the potatoes with the brandy and flavor.

White Potato Pudding

Is made in the same way, with the addition of a $\frac{1}{4}$ of a pound more sugar.

Cheese Cake Pudding.

1 pint of milk, (sweet,) 12 whole eggs, $\frac{1}{2}$ pound of butter, $\frac{1}{4}$ pound of sugar.

Brandy, rose water and cinnamon flavor to taste. To make the cheese or curd, boil the milk, and while boiling beat light 6 of the eggs and stir into it. Boil until well curdled. Beat the butter and sugar light, whip up the remaining 6 eggs, and stir them and the curd into the butter and sugar. Now flavor to taste.

These Puddings are baked on deep pie plates, bottomed with puff pastry, but not covered.

Mince Meat for Pies.

Take of beef hearts, enough when boiled, stripped of the skin and chopped fine, to weigh 1 pound; stripped and chopped fine, beef suet, 1 pound ; currants washed and picked clean, 1 pound ; seeded raisins, 1 pound ; apples pared and cored, and chopped fine, 2 pounds; citron chopped fine, 1 pound; pulverized sugar, 1 pound; brandy, 1 pint; sweet Malaga wine, 1 pint; ground cinnamon, mace and nutmegs, ¼ ounce of each; ground cloves and allspice, 2 ounces of each.

Mix all together in a stone jar, and let it stand at least three days before useing,

Lemon Pies.

½ a bushel of apples, (green,) 1½ dozen of lemons, 1 gallon of Molasses.

Core the apples, put them in a boiler and cover them with water; put them on your fire and boil until soft; then cut the lemons very fine and put them in with the apples, and boil 20 minutes longer; then add the molasses and boil about 5 minutes, stiring all the time, or they may scorch.

Egg Custard.

1 pound of pulverized sugar, 8 whole eggs, 1 quart sweet milk.

Whip the eggs and sugar together, when well mixed stir in the milk, bake either in pie plates with crust on the bottom and raised rim, or in cups buttered.

Boston Cream Puffs.

To make the crust or shell: take 1 pint of water, 6 ounces of butter, 12 whole eggs, 1 pound of flour.

Put the water and butter together in a pan, set the pan on the fire and let it boil until the butter all dissolves, then stir in the flour to make dough. Take it from the fire and stir in your eggs, 3 or 4 at a time, to make a batter. Lay it out on lightly greased pans, with a dessert spoon, about the size of a silver dollar and bake in a brisk oven; when baked cut a slit in the side of each of the puffs with a sharp knife.

Cream Puff Filling.

1 quart of sweet milk, 8 whole eggs, 6 ounces of Sugar, 4 ounces of flour and the grated rind of 1 lemon.

Mix the eggs, sugar and flour together in a stew pan, also lemon rind, then stir in the milk. Put it on the fire and let it boil till it thickens—be sure and stir it all the time it is boiling or it will burn. When it is cold put it in your puffs with a tea spoon.

Cream Pies.

Are made by putting a spoonful of the Puff Filling, in the centre of a three-inch square piece of Puff Pastry, and about ⅛ of an inch thick; turn the four corners over into the centre, and bake in a brisk oven.

JELLIES.

Calf's Foot Jelly.

Take two sets of calves' feet, wash them well, put them in a boiler, and cover them with water ; put them on a fire and boil them for six or eight hours, or until all the bones are stripped off their sinews ; pass them through a colander, set the liquor away to cool; when cold skim all the fat off it, take the jelly, which should be about 2 quarts, and put it in your copper kettle, and add to it 2 quarts of water, 2 pounds of crushed sugar, the rind of 4 lemons, and the juice of 8 ; the whites of 6 eggs, a little stick-cinnamon and chip mace; put it on the fire and stir it slowly until it boils; then pour in 1 quart of Madeira wine ; let it boil up again ; take it off the fire and let it stand until it separates ; then pour it into a flannel bag ; let it run out about a quart, then if it is clear, let it run off; if not, pour it back, and so continue until it does run clear. Be very careful to let no grease or flour in your mixture or bag. Your bag should be wet in hot water and wrung out before you pour out the jelly in it.

Jellatine Jelly.

To make 4 quarts, mix together 3 quarts of water, 5 ounces of jellatine broke up fine, the rind of 4 lemons and juice of 8, the whites of 6 eggs, 2 pounds of Sugar, 1 quart Madeira wine, a litte stick-cinnamon and chip mace. Boil and treat the same as Calve's Foot Jelly.

Brandy Jelly

Is made the same as Jellatine Jelly, only put the brandy in after the jelly is passed through the bag.

Charlotte de Russe.

Three sheets of jellatine,$\frac{1}{2}$ a pint of sweet milk,3 yellows of eggs, $\frac{1}{4}$ pound of sugar, the seed of 1 Vanilla Bean, $\frac{1}{2}$ pint of rich cream.

Soak the jellatine in some water, when it is soft, squeeze the water out of it; put it in the milk in a stew-pan, put it on the fire and boil it until the jellatine is all dissolved. Mix the yellows of eggs, sugar and Vanilla Bean together, and pour into the boiling milk : stir it well for 1 or 2 minutes, then put it on the ice to cool, but not stiffen ; this is the pulp. Take the cream, put it in the beating pan, set your pan on some fine ice, and whip it to a stiff froth ; then pour your pulp into it, have your pans lined with lady fingers or thin sponge cake, baked purposely for it ; pour your russe into it, cover it with a piece of sponge cake an inch wider than your pan, turn it out on a dish or cake stand, and ornament it with icing, or sieve sugar over it.

Maranques.

To make the shell, 9 eggs, (whites,) 1 pound of sugar, (pulverized.)

First pass your sugar through a No. 60 sieve, whip up the eggs light, then whip in the sugar, cover a kiss board with white paper, lay your maranques on it with a dessert spoon, about the size of a turkey's egg, put them in the oven and bake them a light brown; take them off the board, scrape out the inside, lay them on another board, sieve sugar over them, run them in the oven again and bake the inside the same color as the outside.

Filling for the Maranques.

One sheet of jellatine, $\frac{1}{2}$ pound of sugar, 2 yellows of eggs,

Vanilla Bean or extract, ½ pint of rich cream, 6 eggs, (whites.)

Soak the jellatine in water; when it is soft squeeze the water out of it, and put it with the cream into a stew pan, boil it until the jellatine is dissolved; mix the yellows of eggs, sugar and flavor together, put it in the cream and boil for 1 or 2 minutes, stiring all the time; set it on the ice to cool, whip up the 6 whites of eggs very light, and stir the pulp into it; then pour it into a butter kettle or bowl, and set it on the ice until the maranques are wanted. In filling the maranques take two pieces and rub them together until they fit close; then fill each half and lay them together on a dish or plate.

Blanc Mange.

Three sheets of jellatine, 1 pint of milk, ½ pound of pulverized sugar, 1 gill of rose water, 1 ounce of bitter almonds, 1 pint of rich cream.

Soak the jellatine in water; when soft squeeze the water out of it, put it and the milk into a stew pan, and boil it on the fire; when it is dissolved have the almonds rubbed fine in a mortar with rose water, and mixed with the sugar; put it into the boiling milk and boil 1 or 2 minutes; then set it away to cool but not stiffen, whip the cream to a froth in a basin on fine ice, and pour the pulp into it; mix as fast as possible, and pour at once into your jelly molds, set them on the ice to harden or stiffen.

FANCY CAKES.

Plain Kisses.

One pound of pulverized sugar, 6 egg whites. Pass the sugar through a No. 60 seive, whip up the egg whites very light then stir in the sugar, lay them out with a dessert spoon, about the size of an egg, on a board covered with white paper. Bake them in a moderate oven to a light brown color. Take them out and place two pieces together in the shape of an egg.

Kisses can be made in various shapes by pressing the batter through a bag with a tube in the end of it.

Chocolate Kisses

Should be laid out with five or six pointed tubes, and have Chocolate sieved or grated over them.

Cocoanut Kisses

Are laid out the same as Chocolate, but dusted over with grated Cocoanut.

Poland Kisses

Are laid out on greased and floured pans, about the size of a turkey's egg, sprinkled over with powdered Almonds, then dusted with coarse sugar.

· KISS BOARDS should be made of half inch poplar boards, with one inch cleats under them nailed across the grain of the board about two inches from the ends.

Waffers.

Quarter of a pound of sweet blanched almonds, ½ pound of pulverized sugar, 8 egg whites.

Put the almonds into a mortar and rub them to a paste with the whites of egg, then rub in the sugar. Grease or wax your pans, and lay them out with a dessert spoon as thin as you can spread them, about three inches long and two inches broad. Bake them in a brisk oven to a light brown color. Take them out of the pan with a pallet knife and roll them lengthwise on a stick one at a time, the stick should be about a quarter of an inch in diameter.

Waffer Kisses

Are made the same way but laid out round, about three inches in diameter and rolled up in the shape of a cone, on the end of your finger. Have a Kiss Board full of half inch holes, about an inch apart, stick your waffers in them as soon as rolled and fill them with kiss batter, then sprinkle them over with colored sugar. Set them in the oven to dry.

Maccaroons.

One pound and 6 ounces of sweet almonds, 2 ounces of bitter almonds, 3 pounds of pulverized sugar, 18 egg whites.

Put the almonds into a mortar and rub them very fine with the egg whites, being careful not to oil the almonds. When the eggs are all in add the sugar, and rub it in well, spread white paper on your pans and lay them on it with a jumble mould or with two knives—spread it on one knife and cut it off in small lumps with the other. Bake in a moderate oven.

Chocolate Maccaroons.

Half pound sweet blanched almonds, 1 pound of pulverized sugar, 7 egg whites, 2 ounces of grated Chocolate.

Rub the almonds fine in a mortar with the egg whites, then rub in the sugar and grated Chocolate; lay them out on white paper on pans with the jumble molds, and sieve nonpareil or coarse sugar over them before baking. Bake in a moderate oven.

Cocoanut Maccaroons.

Half pound of sweet blanched almonds, 7 egg whites, 2 pounds of sugar, 2 pounds of grated Cocoanut, $\frac{1}{4}$ pound of flour, 7 yellows of eggs.

Rub the almonds fine in a mortar with the whites of eggs, take it out of the mortar and put in a pan; then stir into the almonds the sugar, cocoanut, flour and yellows of eggs, lay them out with a dessert spoon on greased and floured pans, about the size of a silver half-dollar, and about a $\frac{1}{4}$ of an inch thick. Bake in a brisk oven in brown spots all over the top.

Esses.

Three-fourths of a pound of sweet blanched almonds, 6 egg whites, 1 pound of pulverized sugar.

Rub the almonds fine in a mortar with the egg whites, then rub in the sugar, put the dough on your table and roll it out in coarse sugar in strips about as thick as your little finger; cut it in pieces an inch and a half long, shape them like an "S," and bake in a moderate oven on pans rubbed out very clean.

Hard Vanilla Cake.

Quarter of a pound of sweet blanched almonds, and a few bitter ones, 3 pounds of pulverized sugar, 8 egg whites.

Rub the almonds fine in a mortar with the egg whites, then rub in the sugar ; roll the dough out with your rolling pin about an ⅛ of an inch thick, dust with coarse sugar and cut it out in different shapes with fancy letters. Bake on clean pans in a moderate oven.

ANOTHER.—Two ounces of bitter blanched almonds, 1 pound of cake icing,4 egg whites,pulverized sugar to make dough. Rub the almonds fine in a mortar with the egg whites,then rub in the icing,then pound in sugar enough to make a stiff dough ; roll, cut out and bake the same as in preceding receipt. This receipt will make Esses, Blown Jumbles, and Rock Cake.

Soft Vanilla Cake.

Twelve egg whites, 2½ pounds pulverized sugar, a little pounded Vanilla Bean.

Sieve the sugar through a No. 60 sieve, mix the bean in the sugar, whip the eggs very light, and stir the sugar into them ; lay them out on greased and floured pans, with kiss bag, in different shapes. Bake in a moderate oven.

Vanilla Jumbles

Are made from this batter. Lay them out with a star tube, in the form of a ring, and sprinkle red sugar sand on one side and green or blue on the other.

Blown Jumbles.

Four ounces blanch bitter almonds, 1 pound pulverized sugar, 4 egg whites.

Rub the almonds fine in a mortar with the egg whites, then rub in the sugar, sieve sugar over the table, pass the dough through a jumble mold on it in long strips, cut it in pieces about three inches long, form them in rings and bake on clean pans in a moderate oven.

Rock Cake.

One pound fine cut blanched sweet almonds, 1 pound of pulverized sugar, 3 egg whites and the juice of one lemon. Put the sugar, eggs and lemon together in a stew pan, set it on the fire and stir it until it begins to stick on the bottom of the pan. Then take it off the fire and stir in the cut almonds. Lay them out on clean pans with your fingers in lumps, in the shape of a cone about two inches high. Bake in a moderate oven.

Cocoanut Cake.

Half pound pulverized sugar, 1 pound grated Cocoanut. 2 ounces of flour.

Mix all well together so as to make a dough, lay them out on greased and floured pans with your fingers, in the shape of Pyramids 1½ inches high. Bake in a moderate oven, tipping the tops a light brown, also the bottoms, leaving the body of the cake white.

Candy Maker's Cocoanut Cake.

Five pounds of crushed sugar, 1 quart of water, 4 pounds of grated Cocoanut.

Put the water and sugar together in a pan on the fire, and boil it to a gum ball. Take it off the fire and stir it until it begins to turn, then pour in the cocoanut, and stir it well together, lay them out with a dessert spoon on boards or pans covered with sugar. Take a small portion of it, color it red, and place a small piece in the center of each cake.

FINE CAKE.

Pound Cake.

One pound of butter, 1 pound of sugar, 10 whole eggs, 1 pound of flour, 1 gill of brandy, ½ gill of rose water, 1 grated nutmeg, a few drops of lemon oil.

Put the butter, sugar and nutmeg together in your mixing pan, and beat them to a light froth with your hand ; then add the brandy and rose water. When it is well mixed add the eggs 5 at a time; then put in the oil of lemon. Now mix in the flour thoroughly, but as light as possible. This mixture will make a four-pound cake. Bake in a moderate oven.

Queen Cake

Is made in the same way with the addition of 2 eggs, and baked in a brisk oven.

Citron Cake

Is made by mixing ¾ of a pound of Citron cut in very thin slices in 3 pounds of Pound Cake batter, first dusting your Citron over with flour to prevent its sticking to the bottom of the pan. It is baked in a moderate oven.

Currant or Washington Cake.

Take of Currants after they have been washed, dried and picked clean, ¾ of a pound; rub them in ¼ of a pound of flour, then mix them in 4 pounds of Pound Cake batter. Moderate oven.

Rough and Ready Cake.

Take of sweet blanched almonds, 3 ounces, cut fine, citron, 3 ounces cut fine, seeded raisins, 6 ounces.

Rub all together in ¼ pound of flour ; then mix them in 4 pounds of Pound Cake batter. Bake in moderate oven.

Jelly Cake

Is Pound Cake batter baked in tins about as large round as a four-pound pan, with a rim ¼ of an inch high; spread them even-full and bake in a brisk oven. Lay a layer of jelly between each cake. Peach Marmalade is best for Jelly Cake.

German Jelly Cake.

The top is made by spreading Sponge Cake batter on a greased paper on a pan, the size you want your cake, and baked in a brisk oven.

The bottom cake is made ½ pound of butter, ¾ of a pound of brown sugar, 1 pound of fine cake crumbs, ¼ pound of flour, ¼ pound of soda, 7 whole eggs and ¼ ounce of cinnamon.

Beat the butter, sugar and cinnamon light, then beat in the eggs, then the soda, and stir in the crumbs and flour; spread on greased paper, same size as the top cake, and bake in brisk oven; when baked, turn it upside-down, take off the paper, spread jelly on it, take the paper off the sponge and lay the Sponge Cake on the jelly. Ice the sponge all over the top, and cut it in small squares; then dry it in the oven.

Boston Cake

Is made by mixing 1 ounce of cinnamon, 2 ounces of flour, 1 gill of brandy, ½ teaspoonful of Tartaric acid, and 1 teaspoonful of bi-carb. of soda, in 5 pounds of Pound Cake batter. Bake in moderate oven.

French Cake.

One pound and 2 ounces of flour, 1 pound of pulverized sugar, ¼ pound of butter, ½ pint milk, 4 eggs, 1 grated cocoanut, 1 teaspoonful of bi-carb. soda, 1 do. cream of tartar, 1 do. vinegar, oil of lemon flavor.

Mix the flour, cream of tartar and cocoanut together; rub the butter, sugar and eggs very light, put in tne flavor, then mix in the flour and cocoanut, and after it is in have the soda dissolved in the vinegar, and stir the vinegar into the batter; put it in a four-pound Pound Cake pan, or in a square pan that will hold as much; get it in the oven as quick as possible, which should be a moderate oven. It will take about half an hour to bake, and it should not be disturbed until it is done.

Fruit Cake

Is made by taking 1 pound of clean currants, 1 pound of seeded raisins, ½ an ounce of mixed spices, ½ a gill of brandy, 2 ounces of flour. Rub all together and mix in 2 pounds of Pound Cake batter. Baked in slow oven.

Black Cake

Is made by taking 1 pound of cleaned, dried currants, 1 pound of seeded raisins, ½ pound citron, cut fine, ¾ pound of flour, 1½ pounds Pound Cake batter, 1 ounce mixed spices, 1 gill brandy.

Mix all together and bake in a slow oven. This size cake will take at least three hours to bake. It should be baked in a three-pound Pound Cake pan ; after your pan is lined with paper, smear the paper over with Pound Cake batter before putting the Black Cake batter into it. This will prevent the fruit from having a burnt taste.

Buena Vista Cake.

One pound of butter, 1 pound pulverized sugar, 1 grated nutmeg, 1 wine glass of Brandy, 6 whole eggs, 1½ pounds of flour, 1 teaspoonful of bi-carb. of soda, dissolved in 1 gill of cream, ½ teaspoonful of tartaric acid, dissolved in 1 gill of cream.

Put the butter, sugar and nutmeg together, and beat them light, then beat in the eggs and add the brandy, then mix in the flour and soda, and last stir in the acid, which should be done as light and quickly as possible. Bake in a moderate oven.

Butter Jumbles.

One pound of butter, 1 pound of pulverized sugar, 1½ pounds of flour, 1 nutmeg, 6 whole eggs.

Beat the butter, sugar and nutmeg together—but not light—beat in the eggs ; then stir in the flour as lightly as possible. Lay them out on greased pans in ring shape, with jumble mold or bag. Bake in a moderate oven.

Waffers or Philadelphia Jumbles.

One pound of butter, 1 pound of pulverized sugar, 1½ pounds of flour, 3 eggs broke into a half pint measure and filled up with rose water.

Beat the butter and sugar light ; then beat in the eggs and rose water, and stir in the flour. Laid out the same as Butter Jumbles and baked the same way.

Lady Cake.

Rub 2 ounces of blanched bitter almonds fine in a mortar with rose water, 1½ pounds of pulverized sugar, 1 pound of butter, 1 dry measure of whites of eggs, 1 pound and 6 ounces of flour.

Beat the butter, sugar and almonds to a light froth ; then beat in the whites, ½ pint at a time ; when the eggs are all in mix in the flour as light as possible. Bake in a moderate oven.

ANOTHER.—Three quarters of a pound of butter, 1¼ lbs. of sugar, ¼ of pound of blanched bitter almonds, made fine with rose water, 16 egg whites, 1 pound of flour. Made and baked the same as the other.

Almond Sponge Cake.

Two ounces of blanched bitter almonds, rubbed fine in a mortar with one gill of rose water, ¾ of a pound of pulverized sugar, 6 egg whites, ½ pint of egg yellows, 10 ounces of flour. Whip the six egg whites light, then whip in the yellows and sugar, mix a little of the egg batter in a bowl with the almonds, whip them into your batter for about ten minutes ; then stir in the flour as lightly as possible.— Bake in a moderate oven.

ANOTHER.—Quarter of a pound of blanched bitter almonds, rubbed fine with rose water, 1¼ pounds of pulverized sugar, 1 pound of flour, 1 pint and 1 gill of yellows of egg. Put the yellows of egg and sugar in a pan, set them on a fire and stir until they are warm through, then take them off the fire and whip them light, when light whip in the almonds, then stir in the flour.

Savoy Biscuit or Lady Finger.

One pound 2 ounces of pulverized sugar, 1 pound 2 ounces of flour, 1 dozen whole eggs and few drops oil of lemon.

Separate the whites from the yellows, whip the whites to a stiff froth, then whip in the yellows and sugar with the lemon oil, for at least five minutes, then stir in the flour.— Lay them out on paper, about three inches long, with a bag

with a tube in the end. Sieve fine sugar over them, and
bake in a brisk oven.

French Tea Cake

Is made from Savoy Biscuit batter, by squeezing it from
the bag, in drops about as large as a silver half-dollar, on
greased and floured pans; sprinkle them over with fine
cut blanched sweet almonds, and bake in an oven of same
heat.

Citron Shoe Shoes

Are made from the same batter, by putting drops from the
bag of the same size of French Tea Cake, on paper; sieve
pulverized sugar over them, have some citron cut in fine
pieces, stick a small piece in each drop, bake in same heat;
when they are baked take them off the paper, place a little jelly or marmalade on the side of one drop opposite the
citron, then place another drop on it.

Fancy Shoe Shoes

Are made from the same batter, by putting drops from the
bag about 1½ inches long from your bag on paper; when
they are baked place them together the same as Citron
Shoe Shoes. Ice one side of each cake and dry them;
then paint them in stripes or figures to suit your fancy,
with coloring, then ornament them with spinning.

Plain or Lemon Cake.

Sixteen whole eggs, 1 pound pulverized sugar, 1 pound
flour.

Separate the whites from the yellows, whip them to a
light froth, then whip in the yellows and sugar, add the
flavor, whip all for about 10 minutes; then stir in the
flour. This batter will do for penny cups or large cakes,
as well as for sheets. Moderate oven.

Jelly Roll

Is made from Sponge Cake batter, by spreading it about ¼
of an inch thick on paper the size of your pan; bake in a
brisk oven; when it is baked turn it upside-down on

another paper, take the paper off it was baked on, spread the cake all over with jelly, roll it up into a long roll, ice it over with rose water icing, mark it off in slices about ¼ of an inch thick.

Cream Sponge .

Is made from the same batter by baking a sheet the same as for Jelly Roll. Cut it in half, spread one piece over with cream puff filling, then lay the other half on it. Ice with rose water icing

Pacific Cake.

Two pounds of sugar, 1 pound of butter, 2 pounds of flour, 16 whole eggs, ½ pint of strawberry juice, 1 grated nutmeg, and 1 gill of brandy.

Beat the butter and sugar light, then beat in the nutmeg and brandy, then beat in the eggs 4 at a time; after the eggs are all in, beat in the strawberry juice, then stir in the flour as lightly as possible. Bake in a moderate oven.

PLAIN CAKES.

Seed Cake.

One pound of butter, 1½ pounds of B. sugar, 6 whole eggs, 1 tablespoonful of carb. ammonia, dissolved in ¾ of a pint of sweet milk, 2 ounces of Caraway seed, ½ a gill of rose water, a few drops of the oil of lemon, 4 pounds of flour.

Put all together in a mixing bowl, work them into a dough, lay it on the table, roll it out with your rolling pin about an ⅛ of an inch thick, cut it in cakes with a tin cutter, about 3 inches in diameter. Bake in a brisk oven.

Scotch Cake.

Two pounds of brown sugar, 1 pound of butter, 2 pounds of flour, 6 whole eggs, 1 ounce of cinnamon.

Mix the same as Seed Cake, roll them out about one-sixteenth of an inch thick, cut them out with Seed Cake cutter. Bake in brisk oven.

Apeas Cake.

One pound of butter, 1½ pounds of sugar, 2 pounds of flour, 6 whole eggs, 1 wine glass of rose water.

Make the dough the same as before, roll them one-sixteenth of an inch thick, cut out with a tin cutter 1½ inches in diameter. Bake in moderate oven.

Shrewsberry Cake

Is made of Apea dough, by adding a few dried currants to it ; roll the same size and cut out with a crimped edge cutter, about 2½ inches in diameter.

Hard Ginger Bread or Cake.

One pound of butter, 1 pound brown sugar, 1 quart, (dry measure,) of molasses, 4 ounces of ginger, 2 ounces of cinnamon and cloves, 4 pounds flour.

Mix all together and make a dough of it ; roll out an ⅛ of an inch thick, and cut it with an Apea cutter, or make in rolls.

Spice Ginger Nuts.

Three-quarters of a pound of butter, ¾ of a pound of brown sugar, 1 quart of molasses, 4 ounces of ginger, 2 ounces of cinnamon, 2 ounces of cloves, flour enough to make a stiff dough.

Mix same as Ginger Bread, but lay out about the size of shellbarks ; make flat with the hand before putting in the oven, which should be a brisk one.

Spiced or Curled Ginger Bread

Is made the same as Ginger Nuts, only the dough should be stiffer.

Soft Ginger Bread.

Theee pints of molasses, 3 pints of water, 2 ounces of saleratus, 1 pound brown sugar, 1 pound of lard, 1 pound raisins, 5 pounds flour.

Mix all together into a batter and bake them in one-pound Pound Cake pans, in a moderate oven.

Molasses Pound Cake.

Three-quarters of a pound of butter, ½ pound of brown sugar, 1 pint of molasses, 6 eggs, 2 ounces of ginger, 1 ounce cinnamon, 1 ounce cloves, 1 tablespoonful of carb. ammonia dissolved in ½ pint milk, 2½ pounds of flour.

Mix all together, and beat well before putting it in your pan. Bake in a moderate oven.

Drop Cake.

One pound butter, 1 pound sugar, 2 pounds flour, 8 eggs, ½ teaspoonful of carb. ammonia.

Beat butter, sugar, eggs and ammonia well together; then stir in the flour, drop them out on greased pans with a dessert spoon, sprinkle over with coarse sugar and flatten down with your hand. Bake in a brisk oven.

Lemon Cake or Snapp.

One pound of sugar, ½ pound of butter, 1½ pounds of flour, 3 eggs, ½ teaspoonful of carb. ammonia.

Mix all together and make a dough, roll them out the same as Ginger Nuts, only three times as large, bake in clean pans, flatten them down about one-sixteenth of an inch in thickness before putting in the oven, which should be of moderate heat.

Sugar Cake.

Half a pound of butter, 1 pound of sugar, 2 pounds of flour, 4 eggs, ½ a teaspoonfull of carb. ammonia.

Rub the butter, sugar and eggs together until light, then put in the ammonia and flour, roll them about ⅛ of an inch thick, and cut out with a diamond or square cutter ; prick them with a fork or docker. Bake in brisk oven.

Domestic Cake.

Three-quarters of a pound of butter, 1 pound of sugar, 2½ pounds of flour, ½ an ounce of carb. ammonia dissolved in ½ pint of milk

Mix and roll out the same as Sugar Cake, cut with Apea cutter and dock them. Bake in moderate oven.

Pretzel Jumbles

One pound of sugar—B, 1 pound of butter, 2 pounds of flour, 6 eggs.

Mix all together and make a dough, roll it out in long strips about as thick as your finger, cut it in pieces about six inches long, shape it like a pretsel, flatten it down with your hand, wash one side with sweet milk, turn the wet side over in coarse sugar. Lay them on clean pans and bake in a moderate oven.

Fine White Jumbles.

One pound of butter, 1 pound of pulverized sugar, 1 pound 2 ounces of flour, 8 whites of egg,

Beat the butter and sugar light, then beat in the egg whites; after they are in stir in the flour. Put them out on greased pans, in ring shape, with jumble mold or bag, and bake in moderate oven.

Fancy Drop or Bath Buns.

Six ounces of butter, ½ pound of sugar—B, 1 gill of milk, with ½ ounce of carb. ammonia dissolved in it, ¾ of a pound of flour, 4 whole eggs.

Beat the butter, sugar and eggs light; then stir in the milk and ammonia, put in the flour and beat it well for one minute. Drop them out on greased pans with a dessert spoon, about the size of a walnut. Sprinkle a few currants on the top of each cake. Bake in a brisk oven.

Fancy Sponge Drops.

Twelve eggs, ¾ of a pound of sugar—B, 1 pound of flour, ¼ ounce of carb. ammonia, few drops oil of lemon flavor.

Beat the eggs and sugar together with your hand, when they froth put in the flavor; then mix in the ammonia and flour together. Drop them out with a dessert spoon, about the size of a silver half dollar, on greased and floured pans. Bake in a brisk oven.

Lady Fingers.

Six ounces of butter, 6 ounces of pulverized sugar, ½ of a grated nutmeg, 4 whole eggs, 1 gill of milk, ¾ of a pound of flour.

Beat the butter, sugar and nutmeg very light, then beat in the milk and eggs, stir in your flour as light as possible. Drop them in crimped tins, sprinkle a few currants on each cake and bake in a moderate oven.

Rock Cake.

Three quarters of a pound of butter, 1¼ pounds of B sugar, 2¼ pounds of flour, 6 eggs, ¼ ounce of carb. ammonia, 1 handful of dry currants.

Mix the butter, sugar and eggs together; mix the flour ammonia and currants together, and put in the batter mixture to make a dough, roll them in strips about one inch thick, cut it up in pieces about 1½ inches long, pull each piece apart with your fingers, so as to make it look rough. Place them on greased pans and bake in a moderate oven.

Icing or Frosting for Cakes.

Three pounds of pulverized sugar, 12 egg whites, the juice of 1 lemon.

To make a fine icing the sugar should be passed through a No. 60 sieve. Put the sugar, eggs and lemon juice all together in a large stone china bowl, and beat them to a stiff froth with two sticks, about 8 or 10 inches long, each, and shaped like paddles; it is done when the paddles will stand up in the middle of it alone without leaning.

Spinning or Ornamental Icing

Is made by putting ¼ pound of the sieved sugar to 1 pound of icing and as much tartaric acid as will lay on a ten-cent piece, beat it with a knife, spoon or paddle, until it will stand up stiff when you draw your knife or paddle out of it.

Icing Cakes.

When you are icing pound or other cakes, let them be cold; give a thin coat well rubbed in to lay the crumbs, put in the oven and dry perfectly, being careful not to put it in too hot an oven, as it will blister all over; when dry and cold, give it another coat thicker than the first, so thick as not to show the first coat ; dry as before and then ornament it; you can dry it again or let it air dry ; then icing should be put on with a pallet knife ; it is immaterial whether you ice the sides or top first, so as you get it on smooth ; after you have spread the icing all over the top with your knife, you can get it smoothest by drawing a piece of fools-cap paper, or any smooth paper cut the length of the sheet and about 1½ inches broad, across the top, taking one end of the paper in each hand.

Ornamenting of Cakes.

First, to form the bag, take a sheet of fools-cap paper, split it in half, then take one half and cut it across from one corner to the other, so as to form a three-cornered piece ; take one piece and roll up in the shape of a funnel or cone, fill the bag thus made with your spinning ; double over the paper on it so that it will not leak out, place top or doubled part of the bag in the hollow of your hand between your thumb and fore finger, so that your thumb will press on it; place your fore finger on the bag the same as on a pen or pencil, cut the small end of your bag the size you wish the spinning to flow ; work your design on the cake the same as you would on paper with pen or pencil—practice makes perfect.

LIGHT CAKES.

Soda Biscuit.

Dissolve ½ an ounce of bi-carb. of soda, in 1 quart of sweet milk, sieve together 4 pounds of flour, and 2 ounces of cream of tartar, ½ pound of lard, and one teaspoonful of salt.

Put all together in your mixing pan or bowl, work it into a dough, then pound it with your fist, until it becomes a fine, smooth dough ; put it on your table and roll it out with your rolling pin to about ½ an inch thick, cut it with an Apea cutter, and bake on clean pans in a brisk oven.

Spanish Bunn.

About 9 o'clock in the evening, sieve 3 pounds of flour and put it in a pan, then put in ½ a pint of the yellows of eggs, 1 pint of bakers' yeast, 1 pint of sweet milk, mix all together with your hand, and at last beat it very hard ; set it in a warm place to rise over night ; in the morning put in 1 pound of melted butter, 1 pound of pulverized sugar, 1 grated nutmeg, a little ground cinnamon, 1 wine glass of brandy, 1 wine glass of rose water, and 6 ounces of currants; beat all well together, put it in greased pans, let it be about 1 inch thick, set it away to rise ; it will be 2 inches thick when light ; bake in a brisk oven, and when baked turn it out of the pans immediately and ice or sieve sugar over it.

Sugar Biscuit.

Set your sponge about 9 o'clock in the evening, by putting in a pan 1 pint of sweet milk, ½ pint of bakers' yeast, and 4 eggs into 3 pounds of sieved flour, beat it up well and set it away to rise ; in the morning put in ½ pound of Butter, ½ a pound of B. sugar, add flour enough to make a stiff dough, roll it out in small balls, say 12 to the pound ; place them on greased pans and set away to rise ; when light bake in a brisk oven.

ANOTHER.—Put 3 pounds of sieved flour, 1 pint of yeast, 1 quart of sweet milk, into a pan and beat all well together, and set it away to rise. This sponge is best set at noon, or at 6 or 7 o'clock in the evening. When the sponge is light, add 12 eggs, 6 ounces of lard, ¾ of a pound of brown sugar, and ¼ of a pound of white B sugar. Set it away to rise over night, and in the morning turn it out of the pan on your table, and work the same as the others, as quick and light as possible. This dough makes a splendid Doughnut.

Rusk

Can be made from the dough, of the first of the above receipts by making them just one-half the size of the biscuit, and placing them in a deep square pan close together; prove and bake the same as Biscuit.

Milk Biscuit.

Set your sponge about 9 o'clock in the evening, by putting in a pan, 3 pounds of sieved flour, 1 pint of sweet milk, ½ a pint of yeast, and 3 eggs.

Beat it up well and set it away to rise; in the morning put in ¾ of a pound of butter, a teaspoonful of salt and flour enough to make a stiff dough; roll them out the same as Sugar Biscuit, lay them on the pans so that when they rise they won't touch one another; dock or prick them with a fork before setting to rise. Bake in a brisk oven to a very light brown color on the top.

German Doughnuts.

Two ounces of butter, 10 ounces of B sugar, 3 eggs, ½ an ounce of bi-carb. soda, ⅓ ounce bi-carb. ammonia dissolved in 1 pint of sweet milk, 2 pounds of flour, and a few drops of oil of lemon flavor.

Rub the butter, sugar and eggs together, then put in the milk and flavor, then add the flour, lay the dough on your table and roll it out with your rolling pin about an ⅛ of an inch thick, cut them out in rings with a tin cutter made on purpose, and fry in clean, hot lard.

COMMON CAKES.

Cup Cake.

Rub together ½ à pound of butter and 1 pound of B sugar. Then put in 8 eggs and ½ a pint of sweet milk, into which you have dissolved 1 ounce of salaratus and ¼ of an ounce of carb. ammonia, then stir in lightly 1 pound of flour. Bake in Queen Cake molds or patty-pans, in a brisk oven.

York Jumbles.

Rub together 1 pound of butter and 1¼ pounds of B sugar. Then put in 6 eggs and ½ pint of sweet milk, into which you have dissolved ½ an ounce of carb. ammonia; then mix in 2 pounds of flour, pass it through a Star Jumble mold in ring shape, on greased pans and bake in brisk oven.

Rough and Readys

Are made by adding ½ a pound more flour to the York Jumble dough, dust your table with flour, pass it through the Jumble mold on the table in long strips, cut them in pieces as long as your finger, place on greased pans, and bake in same heat.

New York or Poor Man's Pound Cake.

Beat together very light, ¾ of a pound of butter and 1 pound of B sugar, then beat in 6 eggs and 1 pint of milk, sweet or sour, into which you have dissolved ½ of an ounce of bi-carb. of soda; then mix in well 2 pounds of flour. Bake in one-pound Pound Cake pans, in a moderate oven.

New York Fancies

Are made from this batter, by baking in small square tins or patty-pans.

Ginger Snapps.

Mix together 1 quart of molasses, 1 pound of brown sugar, 1 pound of lard, ¾ of a pound of ground ginger, ½ a pint of water into which you have dissolved 1 ounce of salaratus, 4 pounds of flour.

Put your dough on the table and roll it out the same as Ginger Nuts; cut them off six times as large or roll it out with a rolling pin about ¼ of an inch thick, and cut them out with an Apea cutter. Bake in moderate oven.

Scotch Cake.

Rub together 1 pound of butter, 2 pounds of brown sugar, 1 gill of molasses, 1 penny.weight of cinnamon and 3½ pounds of flour.

Put the dough on your table and roll them out with your

rolling pin about ⅛ of an inch thick and cut out with a
fine Scotch Cake cutter. Bake in a brisk oven.

Ginger Bread.

Mix together ½ a gallon molasses, 1 pint of water with
2 ounces of salaratus dissolved in it, ½ a pound of lard, and
½ a pound of brown sugar, 2 ounces of ginger.

Put in flour enough to make a slack dough, roll it out
with your rolling pin about an ⅛ of an inch thick and bake
on greased pans in a brisk oven. This dough makes a
better cake if made the day before baking. Cut them out
with scolloped or plain round cutter.

Brandy Snapps.

Mix together 1½ pounds of butter, ½ a gallon of molasses, 2
pounds of brown sugar, 2 ounces of salaratus dissolved in
1 pint of water, ¼ of a pound of cinnamon.

Put flour in to make it stiff enough to pass through a
Star Jumble mold; lay thin on greased pans like Jumbles,
and bake in a brisk oven.

Drop Cake.

Beat light, 1 pound of butter and 2 pounds of sugar, then
beat in 12 eggs, 1 ounce of carb. ammonia, dissolved in 1
quart of sweet or sour milk.

Mix in lightly, 3½ pounds of flour, lay them out with a
dessert spoon on greased pans. Bake in a brisk oven and
double pans.

Jackson Cake or Jumble.

Rub together 2 pounds of butter, 4 pounds of sugar, 8
eggs, 2 ounces of carb. ammonia dissolved in 3 pints of
sweet or sour milk.

Roll them out with your rolling pin about ⅛ of an inch
thick, cut out with Scotch Cake cutter if for cake, and
with German Doughnut cutter if for jumbles; wash them
over with a brush dipped in milk, turn the wet side over
in coarse sugar, lay on greased pans and bake in a brisk
oven.

Currant or Seed Cake

Can both be made of this dough, by adding either of these ingredients and cutting out with a plain or fine crimped cutter.

Raisin Cake

Can also be made from the same dough, by cutting them out with a scolloped cutter and placing 1 or 2 raisins in the centre of each cake. Bake in a brisk oven.

Rock Cake.

Mix together 3 pounds of sugar, 1 pound of butter, 2 eggs, 1 ounce of carb. ammonia, dissolved in 1 quart of sweet or sour milk, 1 handful of currants and flour enough to make a slack dough.

Lay the dough on your table and scrape pieces from it with a fork, the size you want your cake ; lay the pieces together on greased pans in as rough a state as possible.— Wash them over with a brush dipped in egg before baking (brisk oven.) The egg wash is made by breaking 1 egg up in 1 gill of water.

Molasses Cup or Lemon Cake.

Mix together 1 quart of Molasses, 2 ounces of bi-carb. of soda, dissolved in 1 quart of water, ¼ pound of lard and 4 pounds of flour.

Drop thin in greased Queen Cake molds or patty pans, and bake in a brisk oven.

Bath Bunns.

Rub together 10 ounces of butter, and 1 pound of brown sugar, then add 5 eggs and ¼ ounce of bi-carb. of ammonia, dissolved in 1 pint of sweet or sour milk. Bake in same molds and same heat as lemon cake.

Cheese Cake.

Filling for four pans: Cover your pans with plain pastry. Take one five cent loaf of bread—it should be stale, cut off the crust, then crumble the loaf very fine, put the crumbs in a pan and pour one quart of sweet milk on it; set the pan on the fire or in your oven and let it come to a boil; then set it away to cool. Then beat light ¾ of a pound of butter, 1½ pounds of sugar and 1 quart of Smearcase, add 8 eggs and the boiled bread; mix all well together. Pour it into your pans and dust it over with cinamon. Bake in a brisk oven.

Apeas.

Rub together ¾ of a pound of butter, ¾ of a pound of B sugar; then add 3 eggs, ¼ ounce of bi-carb. ammonia, dissolved in ½ a pint of sweet or sour milk and mix in two pounds of flour.

Roll them out with your rolling pin about ⅛ of an inch thick, and cut them out with diamond or heart cutters.

Maccaroons.

Mix together 18 egg whites, 3 pounds of B sugar, 1½ pounds of flour, 1 handful of sweet blanched almonds, cut fine with a knife.

Roll it out with your hands in strips about half an inch thick, and cut it off in pieces about three inches long.— Bake either on paper or greased pans in a moderate oven.

Note.—You may at times have some white or scalded butter. Now, it will not make a light cake if it is made up in the usual way. I would advise you not to make it up in batter cakes, but if you can get no other and must use it, beat the butter and flour together very light, whip the eggs and sugar light, and beat into the butter and flour. This is the only way to make a cake of it.

PRESERVES.

Peaches.

In preserving peaches, pick out the largest, most juicy and most ripe free stone peaches you can get; cut them in half, take out the stones, then pare each half; as you pare them drop them into a tub of clean water to whiten, for if you

leave them exposed to the air they will blacken ; when you
have all of your peaches pared, take them out of the water
and drain off; weigh them and put 1 pound of sugar to
every pound of peaches ; lay your peaches in alternate
layers with the sugar, in earthen or stone pans, letting the
last layer be sugar ; cover them over and let them stand
until the next day, then put them into your preserving
kettle, not more than 10 pounds at a time, that is, 5 of
sugar and 5 of peaches ; put them on a brisk fire and boil
for half an hour, skimming off the rising froth all the time,
then pour them into a collander to strain off the syrup ;
put the syrup on the fire again, boil it about 5 minutes, then
pour it hot over the peaches ; when they have cooled put
them into glass jars and cover with white paper dipped in
brandy, cut to fit the inside of the jar ; cork them and seal
over with sealing wax.

NECTARINES, large PLUMS and APRICOTS may be pre-
served in the same manner.

Peach Marmalade.

Take ripe yellow or white free stone peaches, pare, stone
and quarter them ; to every pound of peaches put ¾ of a
pound of pulverized or crushed sugar, mash them up with
the sugar in your preserving kettle, set them on the fire
and boil to a smooth jam, stiring all the time to prevent
burning on the bottom ; when cold put them in stone jars,
with a brandy paper over them inside of the jar cork, or
tie three or four thickness of good stiff paper over them.

Plum Marmalade

Is made in the same manner.   Either of them are good for
jelly cakes or tarts in the winter.

Peach Jelly.

Take fine, juicy peaches, pare and quarter them, mash
and press through a No. 60 brass wire sieve, or through a
hair sieve, then pass the juice through a clean coarse towel.
To every pint of juice allow 1 pound of pulverized sugar, put
it on the fire and stir until the sugar is dissolved, then put
a close fitting lid over it and let it boil for 15 or 20 minutes

or until it congeals ; to be sure that it is stiff enough, take a tablespoonful of it and hold on a piece of ice until it is cold all thrqugh, then, if you can hold the spoon upside-down without the jelly running out it is done.

Plum Jelly

Can be made in the same way by adding ½ a pound more sugar to every pint of juice.

Red Currant Jelly

Requires 1 pound of sugar to the pint. Raspberries, Straw-berries, Barberries and Blackberries the same. Gooseber-ries and Grapes 1¼ pounds of sugar.

Brandy Peaches.

Take the largest and soundest White Heath peaches you can get, put 2 gallons of water on the fire, and 1 table-spoonful of salaratus in it; when the water boils put in as many peaches as it will cover, let them boil for about 5 minutes, then take them out one at a time, and rub them with a coarse towel until all the skin comes off; if the skin does not come off return it to the water again ; as you skin them lay them on a dry towel and cover with another; when they are all done make a syrup of 1 pound of sugar to every pound of peaches, put half a pint of water to every pound of sugar; put it in the preserving kettle, and set it on the fire and when all the sugar is dissolved, pass it through a hair sieve or coarse towel, then pour the syrup back into the preserving kettle, again set it on the fire and let come to a boil ; then put in the peaches and boil them about 20 minutes ; pour all into a sieve or collander and drain the syrup off; put the syrup on the fire again and boil about 5 minutes, take it off the fire and measure; to every pint of syrup allow half a pint of White Wine Brandy, put it on the fire and let it come to a boil ; put the peaches in jars and pour the hot syrup over them ; cork the jars, first putting white paper over the corks to prevent them from coloring the liquor. Seal your corks over with sealing wax.

Quince Preserves.

Take yellow ripe quinces and remove the down with a coarse towel, then pare and cut them into six or eight pieces according to the size of the quinces ; then put them into a pan of water and simmer them on the fire until they are tender ; those that become soft first should be taken out, so as to prevent them from breaking; lay them on large dishes or clean towels ; when they are done weigh them, and to each pound put 1 pound of sugar, lay them in layers with the sugar in stone pans, letting the last layer be sugar, cover them over and set away for one day, the next day put them in your preserving kettle and boil for 20 minutes, then take them out of the syrup with a skimmer and spread on dishes to cool, then put them in jars, boil the syrup for 10 minutes, or until it jellies ; take it off the fire, and when it has cooled sufficiently so as not to split your jars, pour it in over the quinces, place brandy papers on top of the quinces, and cork and seal the jars.

Blackberry Jam.

Take the most ripe and soundest berries you can get, weigh them and to every pound of berries allow $\frac{3}{4}$ of a pound of crushed sugar ; mash them up well with the sugar, put them into your preserving kettle and boil half an hour, stirring them all the time; put them in white queensware jars and cover them with brandy. paper, then tie a cover of white paper over them.

Raspberry Jam is made in the same way.

SEALING WAX.—Melt together 1 pound of yellow rosin, $\frac{1}{4}$ of a pound of tallow, and $\frac{1}{4}$ of a pound of beeswax ; if you wish it colored, put a small portion of Spanish Brown in it; keep it in the pan you make it in, and when you want to use it, set it by the fire to melt gradually.

ICE CREAMS.

To make twelve quarts of Ice Cream.

Take 6 quarts of as rich cream as you can get, put your
sugar into it to dissolve; set your can in its tub; break your
ice into small pieces, about the size of a hen's egg; strew
loose salt among the ice, using about ½ peck to 1 bushel of ice;
put the ice and salt in the tub around the can up to the top;
now take off the lid of the can, but be careful not to let any
of the salt or ice fall into it; strain your cream through a
hair sieve and pour it into the can; put on the lid and
churn the can around until the cream begins to freeze on
the sides of the can, do not let it freeze more than six-
teenth of an inch thick; put a pallet knife into the can and
cut the frozen cream off the sides; put on the lid again and
churn the can as before, and so continue freezing and cutting until it become thick, then draw off about ⅓ of the
water; fill up the tub with ice and salt again; sprinkle a
little salt around the can on the top of the ice. Now take
the lid off for the last time, and put a wooden paddle, or a
stick with a tin blade in the end of it, into the cream; beat
the cream light with it by drawing it up at the side of the
can and throwing it down into it again, so as to throw air
into it, this will cause the cream to rise in the can until it
becomes full. If your cream, while beating it, becomes too
thin, churn the can and cut it down with end of the paddle;
when the cream is about half beat put in your flavor; as
soon as you are done beating take out your paddle and put
on the lid; break up more ice and salt and cover your can
all over with it; let it stand 20 minutes or half an hour to
harden; then draw off all the water and ice it up again, it
will then be ready for use.

Vanilla.

Take 2 Vanilla beans to 6 quarts of rich cream; split the
beans with a knife, then scrape the seeds out of them and
rub them in a teaspoonful of pulverized sugar; cut the
beans in small pieces and put them in a tin cup; pour half
a pint of sweet milk on it; set the cup on the fire and let it

boil down one half, or until it colors the milk, it will then be strong enough to flavor with ; when your cream is half beaten put in the seeds and then the milk extract. Put ½ a pound of sugar to one quart of cream.

Lemon.

Take the grated rind of 3 lemons and the juice of 2, to two quarts of rich cream ; rub the rind in the sugar before you put it in the cream ; when the cream is half beaten put in the juice. Allow 10 ounces of sugar to each quart of cream.

Orange.

Take the grated rind and juice of 3 oranges, also the juice of half a lemon, to 2 quarts of rich cream ; rub the rind in your sugar ; when the cream is half beaten put in the juice. Allow ½ a pound of sugar to each quart of cream.

Strawberry.

Take ½ a pint of strawberry juice to 4 quarts of rich cream, and from 6 ounces to ½ a pound of sugar to each quart, according to the sweet or sour taste of the juice.

Pine Apple.

One large pine apple will flavor 4 quarts of rich cream ; pare and grate it, then mix it up in your sugar ánd let it stand at least one hour before making up your cream. If the apple is tart allow ½ a pound of sugar to each quart, if the apple is sweet only put in 6 ounces.

Peach.

One-quarter of a peck of good, sound, ripe peaches—half free stone and half clings, or all free stones—will flavor 4 quarts of rich cream. Pare and stone your peaches, then mash them up in the sugar and let them stand at least half an hour before you make up your cream ; allow 6 ounces of sugar to each quart of cream.

Almond.

Two ounces of bitter blanched almonds rubbed to a fine paste in a mortar with rose water, and mixed with the sugar will flavor 4 quarts of rich cream ; allow 10 ounces of sugar to each quart of cream.

Coffee.

Half a pint of strong coffee will flavor 2 quarts of rich cream ; put half a pound of sugar to each quart of cream.

Chocolate.

Grate 3 ounces of chocolate, boil it in half a pint of milk until it is all dissolved, then put it on the ice to cool ; when you have nearly finished beating, put in the chocolate. This will flavor 2 quarts of cream ; put ½ a pound of sugar to each quart.

Bisco Glace Cream.

Make a can of sweetened cream, allowing 6 ounces of sugar to the quart; when it is frozen and beat light, break up in fine pieces some Maccaroons and Hard Vanilla Cake, and beat them into it, say a ¼ of a pound to the quart.

WATER ICES.

Orange Water Ice

Is made by putting the grated rind and juice of 3 oranges and the juice of ½ a lemon, to each quart of water ; sweeten it with ¾ of a pound of sugar to the quart, freeze it the same way as Ice Cream, but it needs no beating.

Pine Apple

Is made by putting 1 grated pine apple to 3 quarts of water ; let the pine apple lay in the sugar the same as if you were preparing it for Ice Cream ; allow ¾ of a pound of sugar to each quart.

Sherbet.

Rub the grated rind of 2 lemons in the sugar, then put

in ½ a pint of currant juice. This will flavor 3 quarts of water ; allow ¾ of a pound of sugar to each quart.

Roman Punch.

To 4 quarts of water put 1 pint of best brandy, and 1 gill of Jamaica Rum ; allow ¾ of a pound of sugar to each quart.

Currant.

Put 1 pint of currant juice to 4 quarts of water ; allow ¾ of a pound of sugar to each quart.

COCHINEAL COLORING.—Mix together 2 ounces of powdered cochineal, 2 ounces of powdered alum, 2 ounces of pearlash and 4 ounces of cream of tartar ; put all in a large mouth bottle or jar, and dissolve with ½ a pint of water; stir it well with a stick.

NOTE TO LADIES.

The batches of cake in this book can be doubled and trebled, or divided or sub-divided, and yet make good cakes, so that ladies can make them of a size to bake in any stove. Cakes that are rolled out, and fine or plain jumbles can be baked on sheets of tin the size to fit the stove oven; have small boards of same size to bake kisses on. I think that I hear the ladies say : "O, yes, it is very nice to make Almonds fine in a *mortar*, but who is going to the expense of a stone mortar for family use?" Now, I will tell you how to make one that will answer every purpose. Get a small round-bottomed iron pot, then a box or a keg with one head knocked out, and fill it with sand or dirt, and set the iron pot in the sand to half its depth, so that it will be solid. When not in use, keep the inside clean and dry, so that it will not rust. Now for the pestle. Take a block of any hard wood, about three inches in diameter and four inches long, make the sides and one end round; in the square end make a hole that a broom stick will fit; then cut the stick off to any handy length, and you have a pestle. You will find these two articles very handy in your kitchen for other purposes than pounding Almonds, and wondered how you done without it so long.

ADVICE TO APPRENTICES

There is not more than one out of every ten employers, who carry on the Confectionery business, know anything about it, that is, they are not practical workmen; therefore, if you are apprenticed to a man of that kind you are depending entirely upon the good will of his journeyman to give you instructions in the art. Now, the question arises, how are you to gain his good will? I will tell you : Keep a shut mouth, except when spoken to, and then answer civilly; a quick ear, a bright eye, ready and willing hands and feet to do whatever he may bid you; keep your mind steadily on your business, so that when you are told to do anything, and how to do it, you will know how to do it again when simply told to go and do it. The "jour" will see at once that you are to be depended on, and will push you along accordingly, when another boy, who is indifferent and saucy, and has to be told every time he is to do anything, how to do it, will be left to get along the best way he can, and will eventually turn out a "botch," never fit or capable to take charge of any shop, and must consequently work always as a second or third hand. You should give particular attention to the oven, learn all its changes of heat, how to heat it and how to cool it to just such temperatures, for the best of work has been completly spoiled many a time by the carelessness or inexperience of the oven hand. For instance, suppose you put a large pound, or square cake of any kind in the oven, with more top heat than bottom, the consequences would be, that the top of the cake would crust over before the cake had risen to its proper size; then, when the heat strikes the bottom it forces the raw batter in the centre of the cake, against the top crust, the crust breaks in the centre, and as the bakers say, "laughs at the crown of the oven;" the batter runs out here and there all over the top of the cake, spoils the looks of the cake, and one-third of it has to be cut away, so as to ice it decently, whereas, if the cake had been baked in a regular, moderate heat, it would have raised evenly over before it crusted on the top. Now, if your oven should be too hot on the top, shut off the dampers and shut the door, and the heat will settle to the bottom of the oven in 15 or 20 minutes. If it is still too hot and your cakes must go in, give it a light swabbing, open the dampers and leave the door open until the cake has raised to its proper height, then close your dampers and it will take its right color.

If you have acquired the habit of drinking spirituous liquors, which I hope you have not, do not drink while at work. Let it alone until after you have left the shop; make that a rule, no matter what temptations beset you, and you will never regret it.

A TABLE OF

WEIGHTS & MEASURES.

DRY MEASURE.

1 Quart of Wheat Flour, is..................................1 pound.
1   "   Soft Butter, is..................1 pound and 1 ounce.
1   "   White B Sugar, is..............1   "   "   "
1   "   Best Brown Sugar, is.........1   "   "   "
10 Eggs, are..1 pound,
2 large table-spoonfuls of Cinnamon, Cloves,
    Ginger and Alspice, are....................................1 ounce.
1 heaped tea-spoon of Bi-Carb. of Soda, is...........½ an ounce.
1   "   "   "   Carb.of Ammonia, if
    clear like Alum when powdered, is.............½ an ounce.
But if white like Chalk, it has lost its strength,
    and will take 2½ tea-spoonfuls.
3 tea cups of White B Sugar, are.............................1 pound.
3   "   Best Brown Sugar, are........................ "   "
4   "   Wheat Flour, are............................... "   "

LIQUID MEASURE.

½ pint, is...16 large table-spoonfuls.
1 gill, is... 8   "   "
½ gill, is... 4   "   "
A common sized tumbler, is........................... ....½ a pint.
    "   tea cup, is...............................½   "
    "   wine glass, is...............................½ a gill.
4 heaped tea-spoons of Cream of Tartar, are..........1 pound.

INDEX.

PAGE.

PASTRY 5–9

Puff Pastry—Common Pastry—Lemon Puddings—Co-coanut Pudding—Pumpkin Pudding—Apple Pudding—Dried Apple Flourendines—Sweet Potato Pudding—White Potato Pudding—Cheese Cake Pudding—Mince Meat for Pies—Lemon Pies—Egg Custard—Boston Cream Puffs—Cream Puff Filling—Cream Pies.

JELLIES, &C.. 9–11

Calf's Foot Jelly—Jelatine Jelly—Brandy Jelly—Charlotte de Russe—Maranques—Maranque Filling—Blanc Mange.

FANCY CAKES 11–15

Plain Kisses—Chocolate Kisses—Cocoanut Kisses—Poland Kisses—Kiss Boards—Waffers—Waffer Kisses—Maccaroons—Chocolate Maccaroons—Cocoanut Maccaroons—Esses—Hard Vanilla Cake—Soft Vanilla Cake Vanilla Jumbles—Blown Jumbles—Rock Cake—Cocoanut Cake—Candy Makers' Cocoanut Cake.

FINE CAKES..15–21

Pound Cake—Queen Cake—Citron Cake—Currant or Washington Cake—Rough and Ready Cake—Jelly Cake—German Jelly Cake—Boston Cake—French Cake—: Fruit Cake—Black Cake—Buena Vista Cake—Butter Jumbles—Waffer or Philadelphia Jumbles—Lady Cake—Almond Sponge Cake—Savoy Biscuit or Lady Fingers—French Tea Cake—Citron Shoe Shoes—Fancy Shoe Shoes—Plain or Lemon Cake—Jelly Roll Cake—Cream Sponge Cake—Pacific Cake.

PLAIN CAKES..21–25

Seed Cake—Scotch Cake—Apeas Cake—Shrewsberry Cake—Hard Ginger Bread or Cake—Spice Ginger Nuts—Spice or Curled Ginger Bread or Cake—Soft Ginger Bread or Cake—Molasses Pound Cake—Drop Cake—Lemon Cake or Snapp—Sugar Cake—Domestic Cake—Pretzel Jumbles—Fine White Jumbles—Fancy Drop or Bath Bunns—Fancy Sponge Drops—Lady Fingers—Rock Cake.

ICING AND ORNAMENTING..25–26

Icing or Frosting for Cakes—Spinning or Ornamental Icing—Icing off Cakes—Ornamenting of Cakes.

LIGHT CAKES...26–28

Soda Biscuit—Spanish Bunn—Sugar Biscuit—Rusk—Milk Biscuit—German Doughnuts.

COMMON CAKES...28–32

Cup Cake—York Jumbles—Rough and Readys—New York or Poor Man's Pound Cake—New York Fancies—Ginger Snapps—Scotch Cake—Ginger Bread—Brandy Snapps—Drop Cake—Jackson Cake or Jumbles—Currant or Seed Cake—Raisin Cake—Rock Cake—Molasses Cup or Lemon Cake—Bath Buns—Cheese Cake—Apeas—Maccaroons.

PRESERVES...32–35

Peaches—Peach Marmalade—Plum Marmalade—Peach Jelly—Plumb Jelly—Red Currant Jelly—Raspberry Jelly—Strawberry Jelly—Barberry Jelly—Blackberry Jelly—Gooseberry Jelly—Grape Jelly—Brandy Peaches—Quince Preserves—Blackberry Jam—Raspberry Jam—Sealing Wax.

ICE CREAMS..36–38

Vanilla—Lemon—Orange—Strawberry—Pine Apple—Peach—Almond—Coffee—Chocolate—Bisco Glace Cream.

WATER ICES 38–39

Orange—Pine Apple—Sherbet—Roman Punch—Currant—Cochineal Coloring.

NOTE TO LADIES...40

ADVICE TO APPRENTICES...40–41

TABLE OF WEIGHTS AND MEASURES...42

www.ingramcontent.com/pod-product-compliance
Lightning Source LLC
Chambersburg PA
CBHW021440090426
42739CB00009B/1568